CW01430368

Copyright © 1994, 2010 by Simbo Olorunfemi.

First Published, 2003.

Second Edition

ISBN 978-978-32222-3-6

Request to the Publisher for permission should be addressed to :

HoofbeatDotCom
Ikeja,
Lagos
Nigeria.
+234-1-792 1318, +234-1-773 4004, +234 -1-744 4704
e : info@hoofbeatpublishers.com
w: www.hoofbeatpublishers.com

Distributed exclusively in Nigeria by Ikeja Bookshops™
www.ikejabookshopsnigeria.com

SimboOlorunfemi

èkó ree

The Many Faces of Lagos

Dedication

It is for the sake of days ahead of our years
that we share dreams.
It is for the dreams that they shared and left with us
that this work is fondly dedicated to the memory
of my beautiful Mum - Esther Folake Olorunfemi
and my beloved brother - Temitope Olanrewaju Olorunfemi
who left before the dreams had been fully realised.

You live on, in the lives you touched
and the sacrifices you made for many.

eko ree

The Many Faces of Lagos

Concept/Design	:	Simbo Olorunfemi/Emmanuel Umoren
Layout	:	Emmanuel Umoren
Illustration	:	Wole Lagunju
Photography`	:	Simbo Olorunfemi
		Lagos State Governor's Office
Simbo's portrait	:	Ade Plumptre
Editorial	:	Edward Samuel
		Oluwafemi Abolade
		Babatunde Yaya

Appreciation

His Excellency, Babatunde Raji Fashola, SAN
The Governor, Lagos state

Princess Adenrele Adeniran Ogunsanya
Secretary to the State Government, Lagos state

Mr. Hakeem Bello
Senior Special Assistant (Media) to Governor of Lagos State

Mr Shina Elegbede
General Manager, Lagos State Council of Arts & Culture

Mr S. Olanipekun Olorunfemi
Chief + Mrs Oluyomi Ladeinde & family
Barrister Ifeoluwa & Margaret Olorunfemi
Pastor Stephen & Atinuke Babalola
Rev. Chris Okotie
Mr & Mrs Tunde Yusuf
Dr Bode Olajumoke
Ambassador Segun Olusola
Oladunni Ladeinde
Olakunle Tejuosho
Gbolahan Yishawu
Babafemi Ojudu
Fela & Nnenna Binutu
Mr Sami Oki
Folu Oguntona
Femi Ayo-Famola
Lucie Adebari
Shina Ashogbon
The Abolades
The Fagbohuns
al-rarzack olaegbe
Barrister Rose Odiete
Dr Kike Adegbite
Mohammed Yusuf II
Omar Gambari
Biodun Kadri
Mr. S.O. Fadiya

Tribute

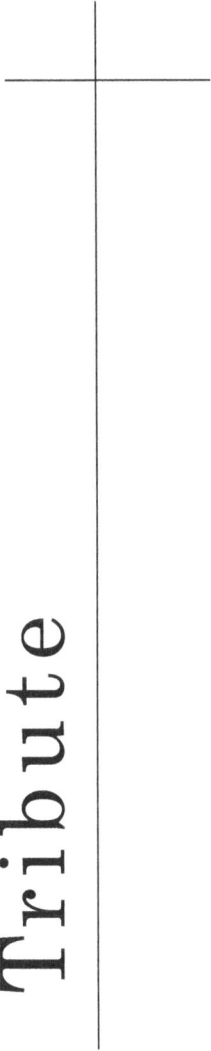

EKO REE is less
a statement
to man's ingenuity
and acknowledged creativity
than a testament
to the omniscience
of the Infinite.

It is a tribute
to the all-knowing one
who has touched my soul
with the longing
to appreciate the poetry
in the little things
around us
that make the world
go round.

EKO REE is, with appreciation,
to the LORD
who has always been,
and would forever be.

Contents

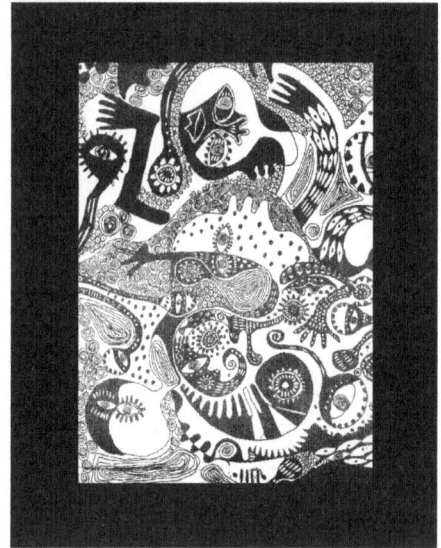

Since I have lived in Lagos for only half a year, my perspectives and impressions of this crowded city in Africa's most populated country are still in the formative stages. In other words, I haven't been here long enough to really develop some concrete biases about the city or its inhabitants, yet. Perhaps Simbo Olorunfemi considered this as a qualifying factor when he asked me to read his collection of poems entitled "Eko Ree". In addition, I am also able to add a "foreigner's" reaction to the collection, since I am not Nigerian.

I believe that Simbo has magnificently captured the pulse of life of the city in his collection. He notices the usually unnoticed and interprets the street life vividly and uniquely. He presents the reader with a delightful mixture of complex and simple, abstract and concrete, urban conversations that challenge us to examine our very being and relationship with our total environment– socio-economic and political. He bathes the reader with the voracity of the city, its people and politics. He underscores our mutual fears, fantasies, and struggles in our daily journeys and cleverly conveys our collective suffering by repeatedly telling us that we shall meet in the "belly" of the "molue", "funky train", "bolekajas", or "refuse". Inspite of our situation, he reminds us that "home is that place where the wind of fate has chosen to blow our feet."

The vibrations of the city have touched Simbo's soul and because he has graciously allowed us to share his journey from one end of the city to the other, the citizens of Nigeria– and the world– are all the richer for it. May your pen never dry.

Dr. Ambrocio Lopez, Ph.D
Assistant Cultural Affairs Officer
United States Information Service,
Broad Street,
Lagos

A Song for Lagos

Using poems to reflect on the life of a city is an age-old practice. Poets, like musicians, have used their art to speak to us and for us concerning our environment. This has been the case from the time of our traditional societies when art in its various forms was created and enjoyed in the context of the social life.

Recently, I have come across collections of poems by some of the world's best loved writers, devoted entirely to the praise of town and country.

Simbo Olorunfemi's collection of poetry reflecting on Eko (Lagos) and its many faces is therefore, in very good company. He has displayed an intimate knowledge of our city, a place we all love. His tone and style is one of simple speech, and I believe this is one reason the work he has done on the city should be accessible to very many people. Simbo Olorunfemi will be judged by how the individual who reads the poems will respond to his special brand of literature. He will be judged, kindly I hope, by many who live in the city and the countless number in whose hearts the city lives.

From the title, the book promises to celebrate the city and this it does so well. Underlying is the bite of social criticism, the same bite of satire that we have come to associate with some of the very thoughtful cartoons of our Lagos tabloids. It is possible that Simbo has been directly or indirectly possibly influenced by the cartoon tradition of the newspapers. This is evidenced by his generous use of picturesque drawing schemes and illustrations that run the length of the whole book.

I find this book interesting and worthy of our support because Simbo's random commentaries on Lagos ring true. But we are glad to observe that, the poems were mostly written before the turn of the century. As such, many who read the poems and the problems he describes will testify that it is indeed a bygone phase in the life of our city.

Development both during and immediately preceding our administration have overtaken the shortcomings. This is a new phase that we are proud of. A process we have been able to begin and which we believe still has quite a distance to go.

I am therefore happy to introduce the book and commend it as an opportunity to view for possibly one last time, the face of Lagos as we once knew it. It will help to impress on us all that the place to go from here is not backward, but forward. And with this kind of love and commitment to our land and country, I believe we will get there.

BABATUNDE RAJI FASHOLA (SAN)
GOVERNOR OF LAGOS STATE

EKO REE
The many songs on the lips of Lagos

Orin tuntun

The bus stop has given me another song.

With whom do I share it?
With whom do I dance
to the rhythm
of the night market?

The bus stop
has given me
another song

With whom do I hum
to the horn of the molue
meandering through its cargoes?

The bus stop
has given me
a song

Let all those with ears
gather their ears
and hop into the molue
so that we can share
a new song
with boli and agbo-jedi

The bus stop
has given me
another song

Something to take
to CMS
and share with the crowd
there

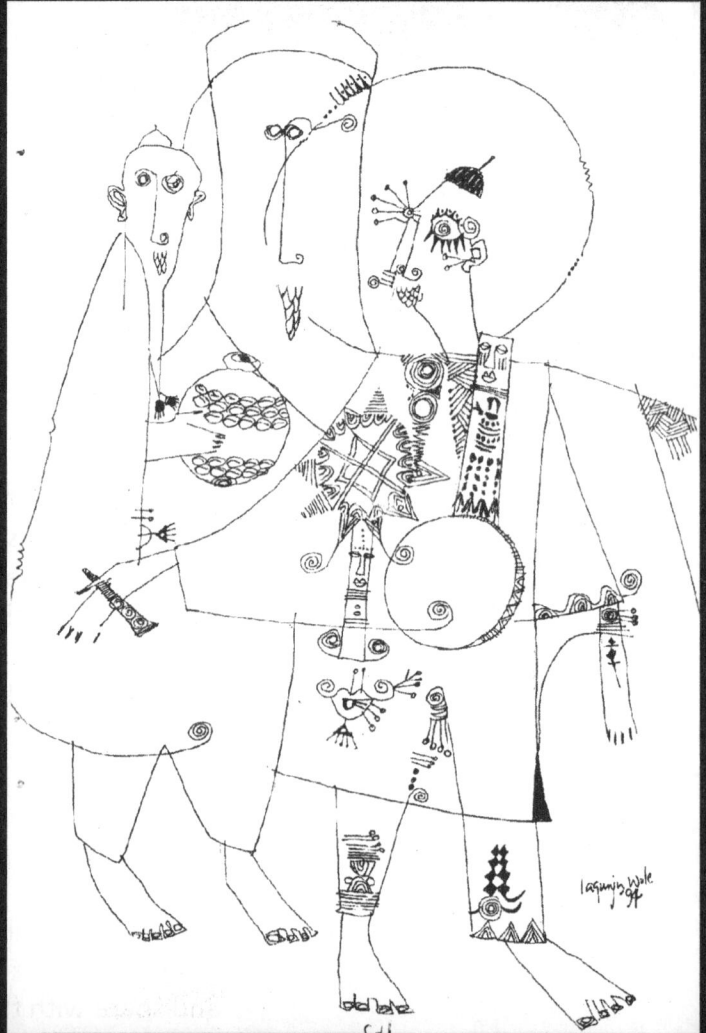

Orin tuntun

I have a song
to share with them
at Ajegunle and Oshodi

before gathering
with the learned ones
at the Lagoon front

The bus stop
has given me
a song
a song - a terror
to the ears
of tyrants

The bus stop
has given me
a song
to plant
in the heart
of Lagos

.

Not even
the extraction
of the wisdom tooth
would stop me
from taking this one
to abe-igi
to share
with the faithfuls

The Madman at
Obalende

I am the madman
at Obalende.

When I laugh heartily
They laugh too.
But they only laugh
to themselves, ensconced
in the solitude
of the owner's corner.

When I cry,
They steal a glance
at my tears
and quickly turn
away.

I laugh too.
Yes, I do.

I laugh
from the heart.
A heart of stone,
stoned to death
by a knowledge
of their atrocities

I laugh
And they say
to themselves
that I'm mad

The Madman at
Obalende

Was I at Bar beach
last night?
Did I
or did I not speak
to the sea
before the waves carried me
atop the mountain
with Lagos underneath

I looked
I wept
And I laughed

I've not stopped
laughing still

I would take
this laughter
in the interim
to NTA
so they can share it
with their thirty million.

So that
those on the rock
can laugh too.

eko rec The Many Faces of Lagos

I laugh
to myself
and the birds.

I laugh
at the innocence
of the evening breeze.

Once, I used to share
smiles with the unborn
in the comfort of the womb
But their mothers
now flee from me.

They all say
that I'm mad.

I'm mad indeed.
And I shed tears
in my heart
for these flowers
parading the streets
in mini-skirts
unprepared for tomorrow.

Ara-Oke

In the thick
of the jungle
back home
we dreamt

Escorting cock-crow
to the stream
beneath the hill
we dreamt

Facing the east,
hoes sitting
on our drooping shoulders
we dreamt

Sharing lunar tales
at the foot
of the dogoyaro tree
we dreamt

einfra The Many Faces of Lagos

We dreamt
of the land
of assorted sky-kissers;
the island
with a bevy of glittering horses

We dreamt
of the triumphant return
with bags of cowries
trailing our jacquard

We dreamt
We came
We met masquerades
wielding sticks
at the toll-gate
daring us to dream.

Eko Ree

They came,
hands in pocket
eyes on downstreet

They came,
lost in the sea
apparent to none

They came,
engineered the rush
cleaned out
and strolled on

They came,
left a pocket torn
tears on a lonely face

They came
for initiation rites
and fled
with tenement cowries
from the new one

They came
and went away,
eyes on the sea
for another one.

Eko Straight

Join me for a walk
at the crack of dawn
Let's chase tomorrow
together
and harvest hope
for our baskets

Join me at dawn.
Otherwise,
the padlock of traffic
shall lock our dreams here
and keep tomorrow
beyond our reach

Join me for a walk
at dawn
Let's go
immerse our grey
in tears from heaven
Let's go early
and witness
the silence of the birds

Join me at cock-crow
let's pierce
the thick coat
of this shell together

Let's go free the sun
and table before it—
the issue of Lagos

eko The Many Faces of Lagos

B'oji, O ji mi

Oshodi Oshodi Oshodi

The conductor's voice
pierces the fog
arresting night at noon
throwing pillows
on the floor
and cutting off
the tree of sleep
quarter to dawn

Iyana Ipaja New Road

The headlamp daggers
the dark clouds
wearing early risers
in the fluorescence
of anonymous rays
sifting dreams
from cold realities
letting ghosts into molue

Obalende CMS Obalende

They troop out
ahead of the 911
on the heels
of a Lagos still asleep
ahead of cock-crow
in search of
stories to hawk about

only to leave
the cowries behind

for at sunset still,
there aren't horses
to show off with.

Oshodi Sha!

Beat me to the east
let's share a view
of the sea
beating towards a heap

Push to the west
and let's see
scattered soles
shoving and pushing.
Eyes on everywhere
heading nowhere

Heads are spilling over
from the choked highway
to the railway
Goods, hawkers, idlers
jostling for space
daring the train
on its home-soil.

Oshodi Sha!

Scavengers having their fill
from refuse-bins.
The crowd- thickening,
and bursting from the seams.
A pedestrian bridge heaving
under the weight of the sea

The molue came-
winners are gone.
The fire, still gathering
strength.

A confluence of confusion
A transit point to everywhere
The centrepoint for distant dreams
The heart of struggle
And the vanity of it all.

Third Mainland Bridge

A convoy of horses
hooting noise
into the still air
of a breaking dawn

Of bumper to bumper scraps
building on the engulfing
cloud of arrested madness

Of coughing engines,
dead to whips
and the madman's siren
slicing through the pile-up

move a metre
pause an hour

Yet we all must crawl
through it all
to the bread-basket

so they named it-
Third Mainland bridge

Molue

But when we gather
our wits together
**we shall meet
in the belly
of the molue**
and piece
our pieces together
we shall wipe sweat
swipe insults
arrange and rearrange
to fill the belly

We shall exchange
addresses
at the back-seat,
buy agbo-jedi
from the vendor,
steal a nap
on the unwilling pillow
before we hit *osa*
staring us in the face

"In the belly of the Molue"

Molue

We shall banter tales
on the fate
of our land,
share scoops from the rock
and ponder
over the mystery
that Lagos is.

All, in the belly
of the molue.

Obalende–CMS

Here am I
in the belly
of the funky-train
squeezed between Iya Oloja
and the medicine-hawker,
drenched with sweat
lost among the forty-six standing
and the forty-two sitting

Here we are
squashed together
praying for life
for the coffin

And the drama unfolds:
See who is accusing who
of not dressing
why don't you go inside
yourself

No change o
I have no change o
I told you
before you entered o
enter with your five naira

The conductor
pushes his way through
wriggling his lean waist
to a barely audible Obesere

And the medicine-man
clears his throat
to dispense
to the dead
the magic tonic
that cures all
from jedijedi to beriberi

Iya Oloja unties her wrapper
and calls for a sample

Here we are
at Obalende -
the conductor
and a passenger
at each other's throat

What is it about?
the crowd-gathering
to find out?

CMS is ahead
Passengers prod the molue on

"Obalende — CMS"

CMS

The crowd is
surging towards the molue
We are encircled already
They won't let it
discharge its cargo

The window -
 the only exit
available

I look back
and I see the molue
swallowing more heads
into its belly

I turn and look
to find the bottle
resting on the lips
of the driver;
the spirit spilling forth
on the tar.

Idumota

I am the heartland
of Lagos
the shrine
of commerce,
the terminus
for buy and sell dreams

I am the masquerade
with the big stick
at the centre of it all
daring dreams
without a spell
in my sweat box

I am the god
with a syringe
into the heart
of the cowrie
the ladder
into the heart
of the island
of knowledge

I am a refuse-dump
for all callers;
for idlers
and weird spirits
who thrive
in the chamber pot
of confusion

Idumota

I am home
to area-boys;
opium-liquor den
to molue-drivers
a morgue
for the living-dead

I am the heartland
of Lagos -
the masquerade
with itchy legs,
the spider
that lures
with cowries

I am Idumota -
those to come
are heavy
with dreams
those here
are pregnant
with questions

I am Idumota
the heartland
of Lagos.

Ojuelegba

I am the eye
of the taskmaster,
the dot
with six faces,
the sun
that never sets

I am the eye
of the taskmaster
Eko of mainland
Oshodi to island;
the centrepoint
of all points,
the eye
with many names

I am the eye
of the taskmaster,
the conductor's
favourite song
the melting pot,
for Area-boys

I am the eye
of the taskmaster
the valley
that never knows quiet
the masquerade
that roars at night

I am the eye
of the taskmaster

Things have changed
Things would change
But not for this eye;
the eye with the whip

I am the eye
of the taskmaster.

Okokomaiko

Now that they have taken power away from the fists of the naira

Now that
baskets of notes
have to be bartered
for a bowl of amala

Now that we have
to empty the pockets
to assuage the anger
of the molue

We can begin to farm
on the high seas
for crumbs
and hunt for crabs
in the bowels
of Dikko

Now that the usurper
has fled to Abuja,

**we must wear our buba
as sokoto
and have chewing stick
for lunch**

We have ceased
being husbands at home.
The higher we reach,
the farther the fruit
we've been longing for.

Now that they have
taken over the fountain
of hope,
what can we do
but pack our belongings
in the basket
and head towards Okokomaiko.
After all, Ajangbadi
isn't far off.

Aswani

And on Tuesday morning
we shall all gather
our harvests
and baskets
in the belly
of the bolekaja

      tie our cowries firmly

      with iro;

      go appease

      the Tuesday god

And they heard the call
back home
And they all came
to the weekly market
with wares and tales
to share
in the heart of Isolo

Aswani

So they all came
to banter and barter
in a mock rehearsal
of the daily battle
at Idumota

It's Tuesday again.
We shall all swarm Aswani -
buy and sell,
fill our baskets
with tales
to share back home

And leave the gods
to take a rest
for seven days.

Oshodi

And came
the talebearer with this:

The wizards
moved a motion,
packed energy
into their wings.
At Oshodi,
they descended.

And ever since
it has been like this:

A gathering of spirits
ever going, ever coming
descending and climbing

And ever since
Oshodi has
not known peace.

But once,
it did rain.
And that was after the annulment

And it happened -
the highway mob,
the railway market
and the unseen spirits
fled with fuel.

And then came
the tale-bearer again:

The wizards again,
are at work.
Feed your eyes,
but not your tank
and fetch rain
from the rock
and see
if chaos
won't be annulled.

Oshodi-
a talebearer's understanding
with more questions than answers.

Ipodo

By six-thirty, assorted tables and benches start arriving.

Soon, hurricane lamps
follow suit
Wares scattered
and wide-ranging
taking their places

The women are coming
chattering up the night
infecting the moon
with their laughter

The buses are coming
bringing in weary soles
and ferrying away
other ones

No-one is
slowed down
by the
threat of night

Why is the yam-seller
going home now?
Does it mean
no one is coming
that might still want
to make the mortar sing?

Does night
ever fall here?

Perhaps we do need
the hurricane lamps
to arrest our dreams
for us,
and fetch us
the spoils
of the Lagos battle.

Agidingbi

You're sweet
the fragrance
is in the air
for all nostrils

You're sweet
And I'm pregnant
with nostalgia

You're sweet
your tar is littered
with sacks of sugar

You alone -
hostess to the fountain
of many pens;
the Mecca
of tomorrow's voices;
an annex
of the cowrie-factory

You're sweet -
wrapped in potholes

Some roads are
dual-carriage ways
Yours remain still
one broad way

You're sweet
And I'm jealous
'cos you hold back
so much of a past.

eko The Many Faces of Lagos

Agbotikuyo

In between
the congregation
of roads
and men
at Pen Cinema;
the unsure steps
of weary travellers
and coughing horses
at Iyana Ipaja

In between
these two worlds
is the dilapidated bench
of the ogogoro-seller
surrounded by pretenders
and retired conductors,
dead to the market
building around them,
and the boisterousness
of salivating customers

In between
the thighs of conductors
battling with commuters
over change
and molue honking
confusion
into smoky nights

In between
a brewing confusion
of vehicles
meandering in
from all points
and the roaring train
elegantly strutting on
with a padlock
on the pervading commotion

In between
the pretence
of tomorrow's paradise
at Iyana Ipaja
and the unhindered
slip to slum
that Agege is

is a square
stolen by inhalers,
daring commuters,
lay-by for molue-pilots
to share laughter
over the bottle
before hopping
into the cockpit

In between
yesterday and today
is the square
and they named it
Agbotikuyo.

Iyana-Ipaja

A gatherer
of weary soles
with distant tales

The last bastion of hope
for derailed reams

The turning point
with multiple exits
and a dead entrance

An ever-present train
of coughing horses
crawling
at snail-speed
to hoots and whips

A meeting point
for the stranded

Iyana Ipaja -
a congregation
of early risers
and nocturnal returnees
awaiting molue's rapture

Iyana Ipaja
a dream once derided -
now courted,
but won't excel
till Baba go-slow leaves

Kirikiri

And soon
we shall gather
at the foot
of the Gbagada dump

We shall dig
into the deep
and fetch
from the belly
of the refuse -
food for thought

We shall soon
be singing
with the rhythm
of the rain

And when we gather
again,
we shall strip
to the waist;
wash our sins
in the morning rain,
annul our past
and share songs
on the dumpsite

We shall soon
be singing
with the rhythm
of the rain.

And when we have
assembled all the pangolo
from here and there
and washed them
in the Kirikiri canal

then we shall bare our bosoms in the rain, cover our middle with palm fronds

and beat
into the ripening clouds
the pangolo
in rhythm
with the morning rain,
away from Kirikiri

Epetedo

Before we can
here gather again,
the clouds must wear
a new coat
we must again
sweep the market
wear the area boys
in new robes
and carry palmfronds
as garlands

Before we can
again gather,
we must fill our barns
with fresh cassava,
fill the pots
with spring water
We must restrain the sun
from going home
fill our quivers
and wrap our bosom
with cold.

Then we can gather
at the market-square
pour out libation
at Ikeja
and head back
to Epetedo,
having seen the gods
down from the rock.

Maroko

And they gathered,
bent on reclaiming
the sea
from the fishes

And they instructed the one at Alausa
to redraw the map
for allocation
to the new gods

First, they partitioned
the stadium
among themselves
Soon, they took notice
of Maroko too
and sent the green ones
to pull down structures
and splinter hopes

And when the bulldozers
were done,
word went round:
1885 has come to be.

But the refugees
gathered the remnants
of their hope
and commenced
on the long journey

And they met
the heavenly assizes
at the junction
who turned them back
to Lagos

With those ones,
they're coming back,
armed with the books,
heading for Igbosere,
to rewrite history.

Area boys

And on that day
we shall all gather
at Iga
with the judgement book
staring us all
in the face

And some shall march
forward
as scientists;
some as wordsmiths
some-keepers of the strongroom
others - having kept time
with the clock
in the morgue

But we -
shall step forward
some to the right
some to the left
A few behind
others keeping watch

Thus we shall put
to the one
on the throne:

Baba alaye,
kade pe lori
ki bata pe lese

May your reign
last forever.

Baba alaye,
father to us all
we are your own sons
without you, baba
we are nowhere

Baba judge
Chief Justice in waiting
have mercy on us
Those who say
we are omo oni-gbana
are the ignorant ones

Baba, let your mercy
prevail
With you, Baba
our case is a considered one

Baba, let mercy flow
so that we - your sons
can continue to taunt
your enemies
with your praises

Baba, we are your sons
we have no other father.

And the judge rose, proscribing sunset.

Oju Ina

Who can arrest
melody
from the flute
of the area boys
when sessions
at Adeniji-Adele
have not changed
their uniforms

Who would dare
rid Marina
of baba alaye
when the rhythm
of the coins
had arrested foresight
and bartered away
wisdom.

Who would win
a free passage
for all
at Oju ina
when today
had been auctioned
yesterday
for egunje ?

Now, we're left
like nuts
in the heart of the fire
to barter
for our freedom.

Oju Ina

Maroko again

And when I come back
I shall don palm-fronds
as babariga
and crown my head
with bitter leaves.

I shall walk
the streets of Ikoyi
in Ibante
and bang iron
on Goliath fences

I shall upturn
the obscenity locked
in the garages
and silence
the roaring sango
in Victoria garden.

I shall suck life
from their pipes
and padlock
their gates
with fire.

I shall squat
at the crossroads
at midnight
and split yams
for the god of rain.

I will take refuge
on the tree
to watch -
to see Ikoyi
swim in the pool.

I would have arrested
their Maiguards
**and seize signals
from the tongue
of their cellular-toys.**

I will now sit
those tingods
on rooftops
to catch a glimpse
of the hungry sea
before the god of thunder
strikes.

Ilubirin

If we have chosen
on timber logs
for cushion on sea
to pave our paths,
on the seaway
of life,
it is just because
home is that place
where the wind of fate
has chosen
to blow our feet.

If we have chosen
to be neighbours
to the shrimps
and share time
with lobsters
It is not that
we don't have
mansions, back home

It's just that
home is that place
where the wind of fate
has chosen
to blow our feet.

If we have chosen
to wean our tomorrow
on salt-water

It is not that
we have not seen
other folks
live on burger
It's just that
home is the place
where the wind of fate
has chosen
to blow our feet.

We knew it
when we packed our hopes
in the canoes
and left behind
the innocence of Ilaje
to lay our mat
on the sands
but now,
the lawmakers
have chosen
to join water-hyacinths
in the battle
for our home-front.

Well, we have chosen
on the shore
to rest our heads

We have chosen
on Ilubirin
to rest our paddles,

because home is the place
the wind of fate
has chosen
to blow our feet.

Go Slow

The sun is shifting
its gaze
from my face.

The clouds banishing
the remnants
of its scattered whites;
heading home
to weave the basket
of nightfall.

How soon
shall night fall?

The leaves already
are whistling
night-time melodies
The fisherman
packing his net
paddling off
to spread its brightness
elsewhere

How soon
shall night fall?

The eaters of flesh
are dancing lustily
to the evening fire
at the refuse dump.

How soon
shall night fall?

My fingers
are twitching -
ready to play
the midnight piano.

My legs
are itching
to discover
new beginnings
under the coverlet
of night
and shower under
its clouds of anonymity.

How soon
shall night fall?

Lagos Rain

You come,
drowning joy
in our sinking shanties.

You come,
padlocking home
our hurried steps,
harvesting tears
on many faces,
floating rooms
as bargain,
for untamed dreams.

You come
spanking heady landlords
on balding fronts.

"Lagos Rain"

You come -
spreading wet tales
leaving hearts out,
wet and trembling.

You've come again?
The homeless
are drained already
of their little hopes.

When will you stop?
We want to gather
out littered hopes,
and go fetch fire wood
for the rainmaker.

Victoria Island

There she is -
adorning the brink
of the ocean -
drunk on perverted riches.

The coy bride
of yesterday,
once sneered at,
now courted
by the rich, the powerful
An unplanned haven
for Khaki-bandits
pregnant from the mint.

A garden - once alluring;
its aloofness
now sandwiched
in between
Architects' transplanted dreams.

Eti-osa-
seized from the jaws
of the ocean
at midnight,
built up overnight,
unsure of its footing,
already chasing the skies.

Eti-Osa-
where would
your white ones be
when olokun
comes calling?

Or have they now
erected barriers
to wade off
the anger of the ocean
when it decides
on widening its jaws?

Allen Avenue

One stretch of road,
grandfather
to a score and ten streets.

A murdered avenue
once quiet,
development arrested.

A skyscraper
in quicksand
built overnight.

Once, only a pathway.
Now rubbing scent and shine
on its twin-neighbourhood.

Allen Avenue
a stretch of waste
and opulence
founded on nothing
glittering at night.
A line-up of white-blacks

An array of tomorrow's cars
with totting cellular phones.

Allen Avenue
fast cars, fast foods
and money-for-hand chicks

Allen-
begging questions
unsure tomorrow.

Nna

And when we
have finally
seen the sun
to bed-rest
we shall lock
our dreams
in the shop
and chase the night
to freezing point.

We shall cover up
our protruding midriff
with silk shirts
in gabardine trousers.

We shall buy
a new fender
for the lexus
and siren
for the pathfinder.

We shall give our pace
a walking-stick gait
and purchase a title
from the capped-one.

Then, we can spill
noise into the quiet
of Opebi with confidence
and night-shift
endlessly
make a pick
at Allen-junction
to dazzle till day break
- no be money?

We shall whistle
into the pub
and announce
to yet-to-arrives
of arriving containers
on high seas.

We shall assemble
empty bottles
on our table
for the attention
of the yellow-babe.

How else
could she get to know
about the three shops
at Balogun
and the new one
at Alaba?

How else
to let the world know
of the mighty mansion
in the village?

How else
to shake off
the odour
of apprenticeship-nights,
surrounded
by spare-parts?

How best to celebrate
the success of our trip
to Thailand?

Omo Eko

Eko is my heart
Eko is my soul

We are bound together
with blood
My umbilical cord
is in her womb
My ancestors
drank from the sea,
so shall I.

Eko is my heart
Eko is my soul

Some we brought here
Some were brought here
They would come and go
We have no other place
than here, as home
We owe yesterday
to this land
I grew up
on the wings
of yesterday's Marina.

**Eko is my heart
Eko is my soul.**

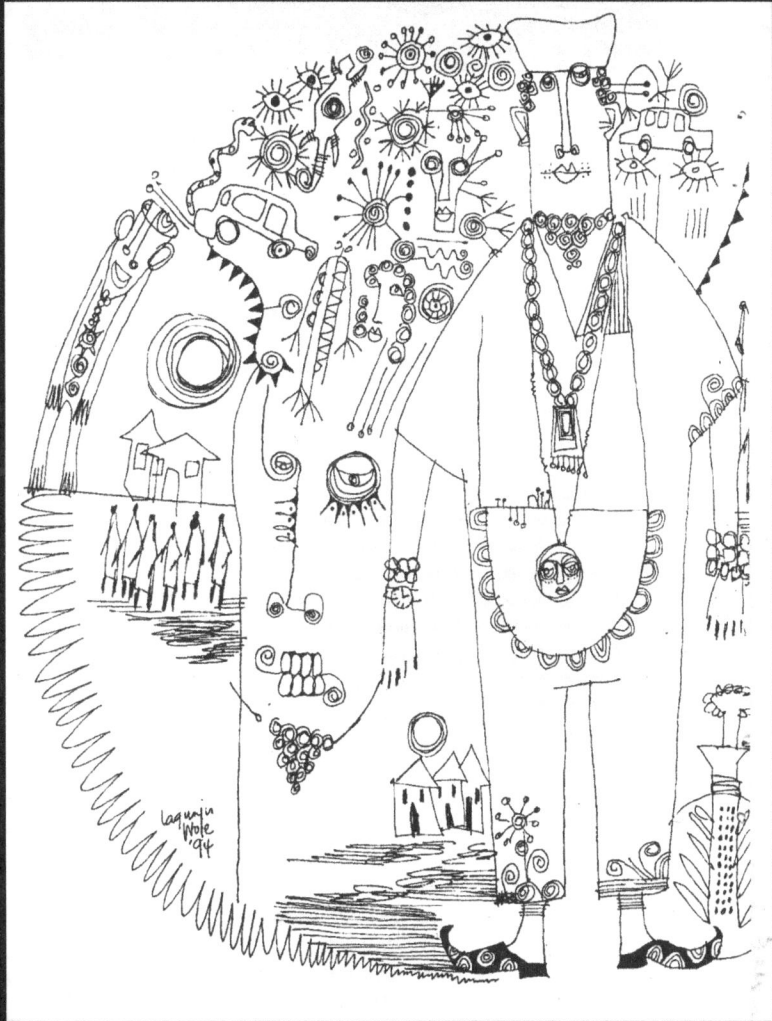

Lagunju
Wole
'94

The sea has been beaten
backwards
They have erected
sky-kissers

on our playground
Things have changed
Times are changing
Eko, yet, remains my heart

Eko is my heart
Eko is my soul.

They can't take
the lagoon elsewhere
where then do I go?
Since Iga would ever remain
the pride
of the heart of Lagos
where to go
to commune
with the relics
of yesterday
but Isale Eko?

Eko is my heart
Eko is my soul.

There is Eko
There is Lagos
We haven't a thing
to say about Lagos
but Eko is ours
and ours only.
We have given them
Lagos.

Eko is my heart
Eko is my soul.

Lagos Housegirl

Sebi I would marry
one day
and bear children
of my own too.

I won't let them
spoil, like Junior
who calls his mummy -
aunty

but sha,
I won't let her be
a housegirl o.

Who say I go born
girl self?

I will born
a boy
I will name him
Jeremiah

He won't be
a houseboy o.
God forbid.

Him go fine sha
like my madam's
husband.

Me - I no go wicked
like that my madam

se, she no know say
housegirl fit snatch
husband self?

I will send Jeremiah
to school
like that kin' one
wey Junior dey go

But how I go get money?
I hear say
dem dey pay big money
for that their school o!

But this job
of a housegirl self.

Maybe I should go
and learn
hairdressing too

But that boy
in the next house sha.
His wahala
don too much o!

Wetin he wan
do self?

I never ready
to born Jeremiah o!

Eko for show

It's Friday,
we all must
go home now
into our portmanteau
and fetch stars
for the night

It's Friday,
Bells must ring
from rooftops
that it's dawn
for another season
of spray and spree

We must keep vigil
in the cold
eat into the heart
of night
wriggle to Obesere
and paste the behind
with mint notes

It's Friday
we must paddle the canoe
into the slums;
block the highway
and shame the brewery
to stupor
- jacquard is it today
aso-ebi for Saturday

It's Friday
the white ones
are out for bargain
we must hit the road
and paint it red.

The kids are home- hunger for company.

Ashewo

In the middle
of the shift,
at the junction
of night and light,
I stand by the pole,
waiting in the cold
for parangida

Along the highway
of life,
with the instinct
of a dog,
I dare the world
to give my trade
a bad name
and dare my anger

Wasn't it anger once
that made me
walk down Allen
in bikini
to inspect
the night-guard
of honour?

Was it anger?

Now I'm in it.
I'm here, awaiting
the night-combers

to come
and deposit
their filth
in the embrace
of shameless thighs

I had shame
yesterday
before I took
a count
of the flock
in the trade
and discovered
I was noone
in the crowd

What of those
on Broad street
in daylight,
only to live Ayilara
with sunset?

Where do I stand
with the Moremi girls,
who have only lust
and greed,
as reasons
to night-shift?

Could it be anything else
but greed
which brings out those ones?

Here I am -
nothing to the world.

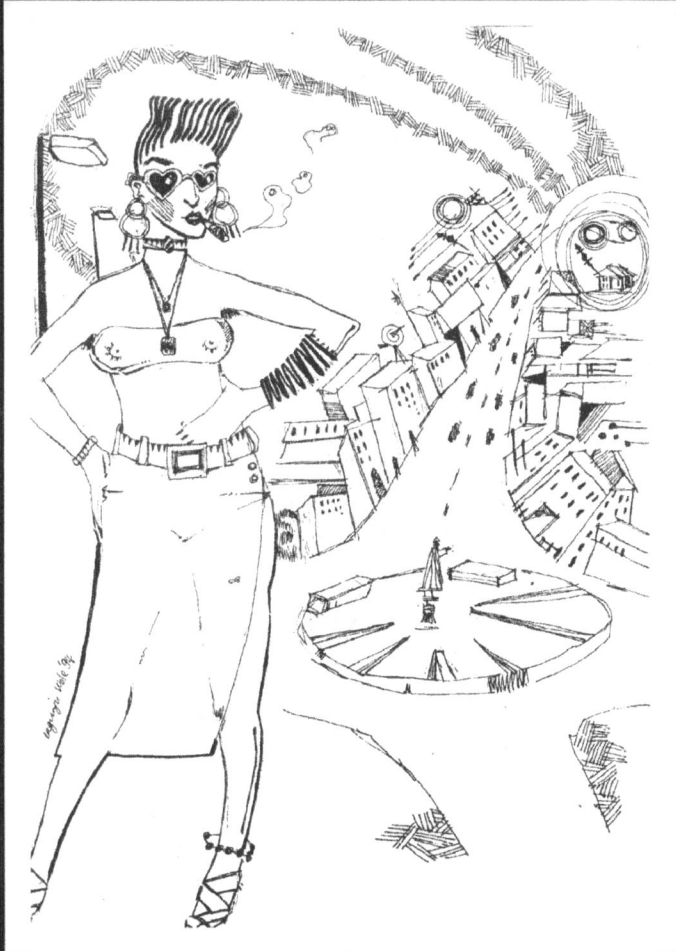

Did I not
take to it
to shame hunger
away
and harvest tomorrow?

Even then,
what's there
to show for it,
compared with those
who do it
in the offices?

What to show for it,
compared
with madam's loot,
for sleeping her way up?

The street lights
are on tonight.

Soon, this facial mask
would fall apart

but how long
would this last?

Sisi Eko

A kid at sixteen
to keep Mama company

I will still go to school
when the harvest is ripe

School could wait
I, too, must get a shop

I will rent one shop
and stock it with wine

I will rent another -
for jacquard and satin lace

Bobo is stingy
Alhaji - my main man

When would he come?
Where again this night?

Sisi Eko

I've not painted my nails
night yet is drawing near

Alaye boys are whistling -
familiarity and contempt

I've bleached my skin
white is holy; white is in vogue

I will go to Mecca
I, too, can do with denture

It's Monday morning again
Where does one go to?

Eko is dull on Monday
I can't wait for Friday.

Ayilara street

I am the godmother;
the harbinger of night
for flesh-trade

I am the centre-point for disguised routes of Lagos folks

in search of nighthawks
I am the hole
that sleeps at dawn
and wakes with dusk

I am the eye
of the taskmaster
with arms outstretched
for skirts
who have scaled the hurdle
and weathered
through the horde at Allen
and the pretence of Moremi
into the warmth
of air here

I am the capital
of the capital of sin;
the red light
that never flickers,
the night guard
that stays awake
through it all
as they come to pick
and drop to pick

I am the godmother
of night itself
the aloof eye
that sees it all
as they go in and come out
as the crowd thickens
and thins out

       I, Ayilara,
       can name names.
       I am the goddess of night,
       the queen of sin
       Soon, it shall thin out.

Marina

There is fire
in the ocean,
yet the other world
is distant
and held behind
by the firm hands
of the waters.

There is fire
in the ocean.
Yes, the sun
has pierced the heart
of the waters,
covering its blue
with orange.

There is morning fire
in the ocean.
The canoes are scattered
abroad,
hunting in the waters
for daily bread

There is fire
in the ocean,
It's morning yet.
All eyes are on
the shrine of cowries,
there is no eye
on the left,
yet the sun
has pierced from above
the heart of the ocean.

There is fire
in the ocean.
The giants are there,
behind the clouds.
But our canoes
are heading there,
to fetch from the pot,
for the sake
of tomorrow.

Oworonsoki

Didn't they despise
you once,
writing you off
as an after- thought
of Bariga?

Didn't they once
think you too far;
hidden from sight
and a hide-out
for the crumbs?

The injection
of concrete and steel
into the bowels
of the ocean
had been written off
as of little consequence.

They despised you
then.
Now they have swallowed
their laughter.
The express-way
has opened their eyes
to the beauty
in your heart.

Now that the ladder
in the heart
of the island
sits squarely
on your shoulder,

they're falling
over themselves
for space
in your back-yard

Did they once
despise you?
The landlords
with foresight
are reaping smiles
beside the bridge.

Lagoon Front

Come see beauty
arrested afar off-
yet so near

Come see skyscrapers
taking a dip
in the deep-embrace
of salt-water

Come hear frogs
croak the breaking
of dawn

Come early
and behold a spread of green
as pillow for coy clouds

Come and dip
your feet
in the warmth
of the lagoon

Come and watch
canoes
take a stroll
under the bridge

Come see fishermen
paddling
into the dark clouds
of unsure tomorrow

Come - you'll meet me
at the lagoon front.

Ebute Metta

Where is Omolayo?
let him come

Let him come
on time

Let him bring
his brush
and record for tomorrow,
today.

Tell him to come
with oil
and stroke on board
the canoes
paddling life
into the lagoon

Let him come
and capture
the huts in the distance,
resting on trees,
reaching out
to unripe clouds

Let him come
before the sun breaks
and paint into life
this green life
in the middle
of yesterday and today
Let him come
and arrest
this beauty on canvas

Tell Omolayo
to come by air.
Who knows -
this one
might soon be murdered.

Abe Bridge

Tomorrow
we shall all congregate
at the shrine
of Iya Alamala
to appease
the god of hunger

We shall all meet
under the bridge
before eight
and slaughter hunger
with a breakfast
of amala
with gbegiri soup.

If Kadi comes along,
we shall crack
the delicate bones
of eja osan
and order bokoto
for the plateau teeth
of Angel Gabriel.

Tomorrow, at dawn,
we shall again
cool our heels
under the bridge;
keep ponmo in reserve
for Toyin
and make panla available
for Joke
Don't tell Papa
that we too
were at abe bridge.

Broad Street

What kind of beauty
is this, that chooses
to sleep
all day long
only to spread
its petals
at night?

What kind of beauty
is this,
that hides itself
from the sun
only to spread
its wings
across the sky
with sunset?

How dare it
keep away,
all day,
when bankers
are looking up
to the skies
for fund?

Broad Street

How dare it
hide itself
while soles battle
on the street
for survival
in blazing sunshine?

Tonight,
I will walk down
to the end of the road.
Go up Elephant house,
into the penthouse,
and ask the sky
why beauty should only call
on Broad Street
at night.

Jakande Estate

I can see your stars
in the far
I can see the twinkle
in your eyes
from above

I can hear from here
your throaty laughter
I can see from above
the glint denied your cones
the day before
When shall I be home?
How soon can I be
wrapped in the comfort
of your night?

How soon can I be safe
in the pit of your arms
and paddle on the laps
of your laughter?

I shall leave the crowd
behind soon
I shall take a flight
above this gathering garbage
and be home soon
on your waiting pillow

I shall be home soon
Who knows
when NEPA's sunshine
will come our way again?

Omoshalewa

Where does this sun
rise
that it chooses only
to sprinkle its orange
at six
on Ipaja clouds?

Where is the source
of this brightness
lurking with evenings
in the shadow
of green
under the tongue
of NEPA poles?

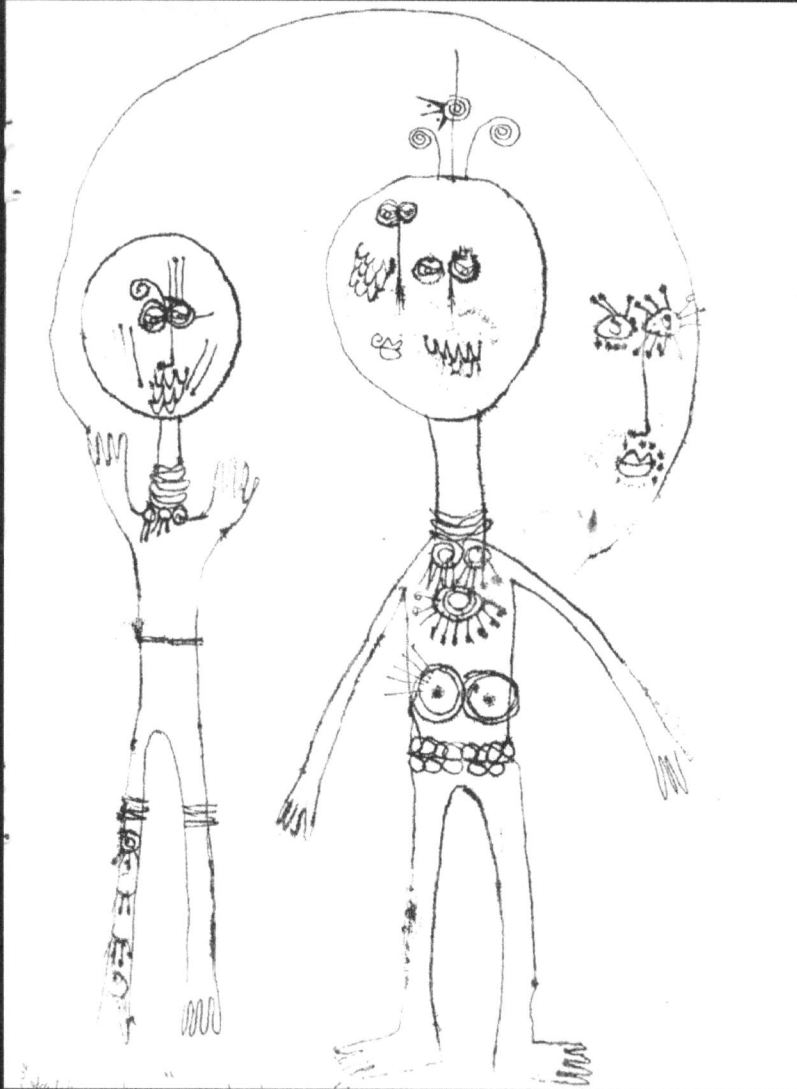

Omoshalewa

Where does this one
take its source,
so that we can carry
our pots there
at midnight
supplicate to its god
to make it
an all-day affair?

Where is its source
so that
we can go appease
the god of refuse too,
to come
cart away its sacrifice
littered on
our potholed roads?

Where does this sun
have its source
so that we can go
rebirth Abesan there
and change its name
from Omoshalewa?

eldred The Many Faces of Lagos

Bar beach

Just as we were
beginning
to spread our mats,
the moon
swallowed its tongue,
leaving behind
parboiled dreams.

Just when
we were beginning
to clothe our nude,
and cuddle warmth
under the tongue
of the moon,
it rolled its mat
across the ocean-line

Just when
the stars were beginning
to infect us
with sparkle,
the moon pulled its mat
off our backs

Just when
we were about
re-immersing ourselves
in Ijapa's well of wisdom,
the moon
arrested our laughter.

Now, we have
to plough our way
back home,
break through
the barriers of night,
leave behind memories
in the heart
of the coast,
now swept off
and buried.

Whispering Palms

I can feel
the hands of the sea
on my shoulder
lifting my worries
from the pebbles
into the crevice
of her bowels

I can feel
the hands of the sea,
salting my face
with a cooing breeze;
singing the old song,
with my own tongue,
for my ears only.

I can feel
rain droplets
on my grey
emboldening the whispers
of the palms
into thundering choruses

I can feel tomorrow
in the palms of today
I can feel power
in the hands of the sea
and joy
in the music
bursting forth
from my within.

I can see the west
neighbouring my dream,
wearing me with strength,
to face the east again.

Campos Square

And when the time
comes,
we shall gather
for songs
at the foot
of the lone odan tree
at Campos Square

We shall share
lunar songs
into the coat of night
in celebration
of a song-filled
yesterday

We shall all come
with gurundi
to spice
the midnight laughter
drifting with the breeze
from Itafaji
and savour
the serenity
denied the day
by commerce
and sojourners.

Ibeju-Lekki

I still would come back
lean on coconut tree
and bath with salt-water.

I still would come back
and whistle in rhyme
with your neighbour

I shall come
with a tipcart
to fetch pebbles
from your shore

I will come alone
strip to the bare
and drink coconut-water

I too will build a hut
by the sea to feed
on prawns and lobsters

I surely would come back
to harvest a maiden
from your neighbourhood

We shall bring
yams for fish
and take for keeps
your mammy-water.

A Song for Lagos

Give me the heart
of Lagos
And
I shall append my signature
on sunset
I shall make a tent
on the bridge
and pass the night
thereon to eternity

Give me the heart
of Lagos
And
I shall plant a ladder
in the sea,
paint the canvas in orange
throw out the hook
and harvest
for your basket
the sunset

Give me the heart
of Lagos
And
I shall perch on the tree
to watch
the day speed by
in roving canoes,
while waiting
on the heels of night

Give me the heart
of Lagos
And I shall sing the sun
to lullaby
and dwell forever
on the wings of the sea
to watch the trees
spread out fingers
on the face of orange clouds.

Give me the heart
of Lagos
And
I shall take you
up the bridge
to see the sun
going home
I shall take you up
to watch darkness
creep in
on empty baskets

Give me the heart
of Lagos
And I shall give you
a peck at sunset,
to hold on to, forever.

Glossary

NTA - Federal Government's owned Nigerian Television Authority

Molue - Purpose-built mass transit truck, peculiar to Lagos roads

Agbo-jedi - Herbal concoction, with purported medicinal properties,
  often marketed as a cure-all.

Boli - Roasted plantain

Abe-igi - (Literal meaning – Under the tree). A popular spot where
  the arts community socializes at the National Theatre.

Eyo-Festival- Masquerade traditional to people of Lagos island

Third Mainland bridge - A major link between the Lagos island and mainland

Osa - Lagoon

Funky train - Nickname for Molue

Iya Oloja - Female trader

Dressing - Adjusting a seating position

Naira - Unit of money in Nigeria

Obesere - Fuji Musician, notable for his racy lyrics

Jedi-jedi - Pile

Beri-beri- Kwashiorkor

Area boys - Vagrants

Amala- Food made with yam flour

Abuja - Nigeria's capital city

Buba - Traditional shirt-like Yoruba garment

Sokoto- Traditional Yoruba trousers

Iro - A wrap-around attire worn by Yoruba women

Bolekaja - A truck with locally fabricated appendage for
  ferrying passengers and goods

Baba - Elderly man

Egunje - Kick-back

Babariga - Flowing outer garment, popular worn in Northern Nigeria

Ibante - Short skirt worn by Yoruba warriors

Sango- Mythical Yoruba god of thunder

Maiguard - Security guard

Nna - Elderly man (Igbo)

Mama - Elderly woman

Kadi - Author's colleague/friend

Aso-ebi - Uniformed attire by a family

Parangida - All-night session(Hausa)

Moremi - Female hostel at University of Lagos

Omolayo - An accomplished Nigerian artist

Iya Alamala - One who prepares amala for sale

Gbegiri - Bean soup

Eja osan - Cat fish

Angel Gabriel- Author's colleague/friend

Toyin- Author's colleague/friend

Panla - Stockfish

Joke - Author's colleague/friend

Papa - Nickname for Author's elderly colleague(Mr Folarin)

NEPA - Nigeria's electric power monopoly, notorious for incessant outage

Ijapa - Tortoise

Ogogoro - Locally brewed gin

Iga - Palace

Places in Lagos

Elephant house, Broad street, Obalende, Bar beach, Ipaja, Abesan, Campos square, Itafaji, Ibeju-Lekki, CMS, Ajegunle, Oshodi, Iyana-Ipaja, Okokomaiko, Ajangbadi, Isolo, Idumota, Aswani, Ipodo, Pen cinema, Jakande Estate, Agege, Agbotikuyo,Gbagada, Epetedo, Ikeja, Alausa, Eko, Maroko, Adeniji-Adele, Marina, Oju-ina, Bariga, Ikoyi, Victoria garden, Ilaje, Eti-osa, Allen avenue, Opebi, Balogun, Alaba, Broad street, Ayilara.

MY PRAYER

Lord, give me a deep sense of appreciation for those little things that make the world go round. Touch my soul with the longing to be rekindled by the fire in the heart of the sun as it peels off the mask on the innocence of dawn; the grace to draw strength from the smile on the lips of the star as it showers brightness on the firmament; the joy of a renewal from the moon as it stretches out its mat for concourse; and the excitement of a rebirth in the cascading drops of the morning rain.

I pray for the needle of resemblance to take its place in my heart to always prick me into the knowledge of who I am; readily cast my mind to the beginning, when I was but a little bundle in the cot; and inject my heart with the humility to keep my head, no matter what height, I attain.

Give me the strength of mind to pinpoint and acknowledge my faults; to make restitution for such; and keep away from filth. Bless me with a heart to forgive and forget; and an eye that overlooks the frailties of others. Let it be given me the time and energy to administer to the needs of the needy - making my society the better for it.

I pray for the patience to wait on good to overcome evil; the wisdom to identify the truth; and the courage to stand, and be identified with it.

God, please enrapture me with boundless love; bless me with a good ear for music; and a life with poetry. Let it be mine to have peace of mind - infectious like a ballad shared between the evening breeze and the coconut tree on a deserted beach.

© Simbo Olorunfemi, 1993

Show your colours

Share your Lagos experience with all.
Bare it all.

All info you need at your fingertips.
Advertise your products and services **FREE**

Visit. Share. Learn.
@
www.ekoonibajeng.com
Lagos forum (That Lagos might excel)

Jobs . Politics . Romance . Entertainment . Consumer parliament

Lightning Source UK Ltd.
Milton Keynes UK
UKOW07f1041130515

251418UK00011B/366/P